ISAAC ASIMOV'S
Library of the Universe

APR 0 5 1990

Astronomy Today

by Isaac Asimov

Gareth Stevens Publishing
Milwaukee

Library of Congress Cataloging-in-Publication Data

Asimov, Isaac, 1920-
  Astronomy today / by Isaac Asimov.
        p.   cm. — (Isaac Asimov's library of the universe)
  Bibliography: p.
  Includes index.
  Summary: Discusses how scientists and amateurs use instruments to study the universe and describes some astronomical discoveries.
  ISBN 1-55532-402-9
  1. Astronomy—Juvenile literature. [1. Astronomy.] I. Title. II. Series: Asimov, Isaac, 1920-   Library of the universe.
  QB46.A78   1989   89-4631
  520—dc20

A Gareth Stevens Children's Books edition

Edited, designed, and produced by
Gareth Stevens, Inc.
RiverCenter Building, Suite 201
1555 North RiverCenter Drive
Milwaukee, Wisconsin 53212, USA

For a free color catalog describing Gareth Stevens' list of high-quality children's books call 1-800-341-3569.

Cover painting courtesy of Jet Propulsion Laboratory

Project editor: Mark Sachner
Series design: Laurie Shock
Book design: Kate Kriege
Research editor: Kathleen Weisfeld Barrilleaux
Picture research: Matthew Groshek
Technical advisers and consulting editors: Julian Baum and Francis Reddy

Printed in the United States of America

1 2 3 4 5 6 7 8 9 95 94 93 92 91 90

CONTENTS

Nowadays, we have seen planets up close, all the way to distant Uranus and Neptune. We have mapped Venus through its clouds. We have seen dead volcanoes on Mars and live ones on Io, one of Jupiter's satellites. We have detected strange objects no one knew anything about till recently: quasars, pulsars, black holes. We have studied stars not only by the light they give out, but by other kinds of radiation: infrared, ultraviolet, x-rays, radio waves. We have even detected tiny particles called neutrinos that are given off by the stars.

Let's see just how astronomers do their work today, both with large and magnificent instruments of many kinds, and in simpler ways. Astronomy is one science in which people who are not professionals can still contribute, even with simple instruments. That makes astronomy even more exciting for amateurs like you and me.

Isaac Asimov

What Is Astronomy?

In ancient times, astronomers simply gazed skyward. In that way, they learned a great deal about how the Sun, Moon, and planets moved across the sky. They also figured out the length of the year and worked out calendars.

Nowadays, astronomers <u>still</u> look at the sky. But today they have new ways of collecting information from the sky, and they have new ideas about how the Universe works. For example, astronomers now use instruments that collect more light and study kinds of radiation we can't see with our eyes. They also know more science, so by analyzing starlight they can tell what stars are made of, how they came to be, how they change with time, and how they come to an end.

What's more, astronomers are always developing even newer and better instruments.

Opposite: A misty path called the Milky Way cuts through the darkness of the night sky. It is the combined light of the billions of stars in our Galaxy. Inset, opposite: Our eyes detect only visible light, but our machines can reveal other "colors," called radiation, that lie beyond the red and violet ends of the visible spectrum.

The Medicine Wheel at Big Horn, Wyoming, was an ancient observatory used to record the motions of celestial objects and, like a calendar, to measure the passing of the days. Inset: A South Korean postage stamp celebrates an ancient observatory.

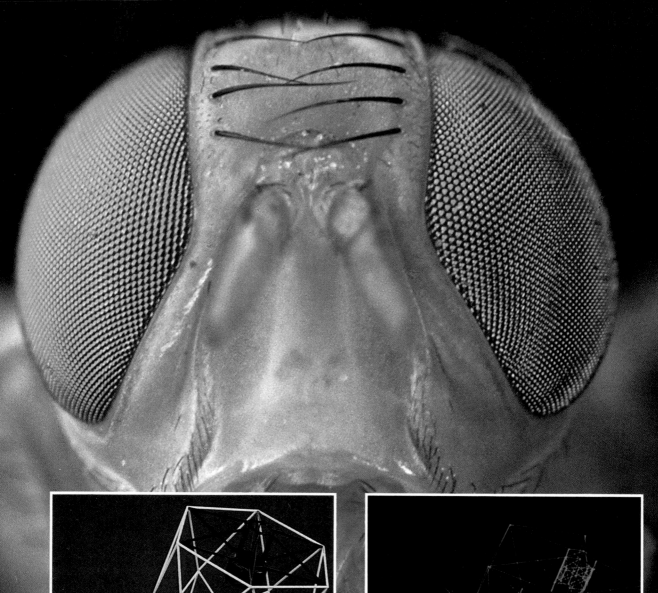

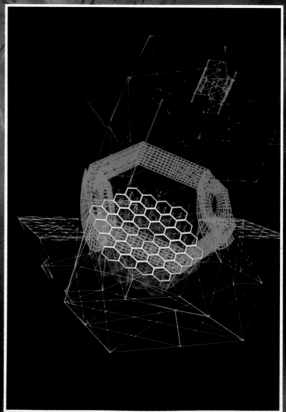

Telescopes of Modern Astronomy

The best-known instruments of astronomers today are the large telescopes. In 1948, on Mount Palomar in California, a telescope with a mirror 200 inches (about 5 m) across was installed. It collects 360,000 times as much light as the human eye does!

In 1974, the Soviet Union built a telescope in the Caucasus Mountains with a mirror 236 inches (about 6 m) across. Now, even bigger and more effective telescopes are in the works. New telescopes have many small mirrors that all work together by computer. And scientists are developing newer types of glass to make telescopes both stronger and lighter.

Opposite: The fly sees through an eye containing thousands of tiny lenses.

Insets, opposite: a fly eyed telescope? The Keck telescope in Hawaii will use 36 small mirrors to create a mirror twice as wide as Palomar's. Left: a model of the telescope. Right: a computer-drawn sketch of the mirror in place.

Below: the 200-inch (5-m) telescope on Mount Palomar.

Above: Workers polish one of Keck's small mirrors.

The new telescopes — getting a bead on the cosmos

Scientists are building better telescopes for use on the ground and in the air. In the case of some mirrors, a vacuum is applied to one side and the mirror is then "sprung" into contact with air, where it takes on its correct shape. High above, flying observatories sail the skies. These specially equipped planes help astronomers view the Sun, planets, and even distant stars from high above the distortion of Earth's atmosphere. More than ever, our "eyes" are on the stars.

A simulated view of a distant star cluster as seen from Earth (top) and through the Hubble Space Telescope (bottom).

The Space Telescope

It doesn't matter whether the telescope you use is in an observatory or in your bedroom window — all telescopes on Earth have problems. Clouds and fog hide the sky. The atmosphere absorbs some kinds of light. It scatters light by day so you can't see the stars. Even on clear nights, the air can be unsteady, causing the stars to quiver.

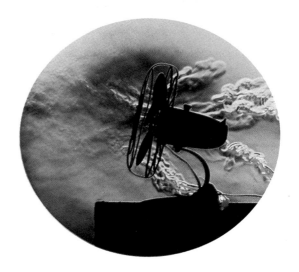

Special photography reveals currents of air warmed by candles. Similar currents can scramble the messages in starlight.

The United States is planning to put a large telescope, the Hubble Space Telescope, into orbit beyond Earth's atmosphere. From there, it will help us see farther and more clearly into the cosmos than you can imagine. It will show us distant galaxies, and it will be our "eyes" peering deep into star clusters.

The Space Telescope will gather light from near and deep space and help us figure out how large and how old the Universe is. It will help us know more about the very farthest edges of the Universe.

Opposite: An artist imagines the Hubble Space Telescope in orbit.

Below: Astronomers place their telescopes on mountaintops, where they can look through the clean, dry air above the clouds.

Seeing by Radio

Stars give off radio waves as well as light, so we have built special radio telescopes that concentrate and receive radio waves.

Radio waves can give us information that light does not. For example, radio waves have helped us detect very distant objects called quasars and tiny, rapidly rotating stars called pulsars. We have also found black holes in the center of galaxies and various chemicals in clouds of dust between stars.

A satellite called the Infrared Astronomical Satellite (IRAS) has detected heat waves called infrared waves. IRAS recently picked up infrared waves from places near some distant stars. These signals may mean that planets are forming about the stars.

Opposite: Are planets forming around the star Beta Pictoris? Many astronomers believe that a cloud of dust and gas similar to that which made our Solar system encircles the star.

Insets: M31, the closest spiral galaxy to us, as seen by infrared (top), radio waves (middle), and visible light (bottom). Each method shows us something different about M31.

Below: Dr. Jocelyn Bell Burnell, discoverer of pulsars.

**Would you believe . . .
. . . Little Green Men?**

In 1967, a young British astronomer, Jocelyn Bell, helped build a huge radio telescope made up of 2,048 antennas. Radio signals detected by this telescope were so steady that people wondered if they came from an intelligent source. For a while, these signals were called LGM, for "Little Green Men." But they were too steady to be of intelligent origin. Bell had discovered pulsars — rapidly spinning neutron stars sending out radio signals with each turn.

Computer Astronomy

Scientists can use computers to make a number of small telescopes work together exactly as if they were one large telescope. Thanks to computers, radio telescopes that are up to thousands of miles apart can detect radio waves more sharply than ordinary telescopes see light.

Computers can also analyze the light that telescopes receive and study it with greater precision than eyes or cameras can. Thanks to computers, astronomers can now see dim stars, remote galaxies, and other distant objects in the sky more sharply than ever before.

Opposite: An array of small radio telescopes can be electronically combined to function as one "superscope." Inset: An astronomer studies an image produced by radio telescopes.

Right: A network of radio telescopes could be linked to create an Earth-sized antenna.

Below: the Very Large Array of radio telescopes in Socorro, New Mexico. Each arm of the VLA is 13 miles (21 km) long.

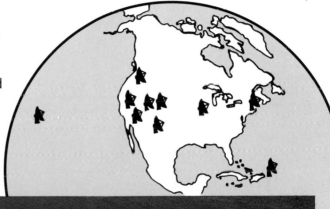

Gazing into the Past

As we see objects that are farther and farther off in space, we also see them as they existed longer and longer ago. Traveling at about 186,000 miles (300,000 km) per second, light from the nearest star other than our Sun takes over four years to reach us.

Light from two nearby galaxies, the Magellanic clouds, takes over 150,000 years to reach us. Light from the Andromeda Galaxy, another galactic neighbor, takes over two million years to get here.

Quasars are distant objects with very bright centers. We see them by light that left them from one to ten billion years ago. Our best instruments can see galaxies by the light that left them 17 billion years ago. This tells us something about how old the Universe might be and the way in which it developed after it came into being.

> ## 1987A — our "neighborly" supernova
>
> *Every once in a while a star explodes and briefly shines with the light of a billion ordinary stars. For nearly 400 years, since 1604, not a single supernova has appeared in our Galaxy — only in distant ones. So with all our fancy instruments, we were not able to study supernovas up close — until 1987, when a supernova appeared in the Large Magellanic Cloud, a galaxy just next door. At last astronomers could study a supernova that was fairly close by.* ●

Above: Supernova 1987A (bright spot, left) in the Large Magellanic Cloud.

Above: Moonlight takes over a second to reach us. If you bounced a flashlight beam off the Moon, the light would take about 1.3 seconds to reach the Moon — and another 1.3 seconds to bounce back to your eye!

Opposite: A diver works inside a water-filled particle detector. Over 2,000 sensitive light sensors watch for the telltale flashes that occur when particles called neutrinos are captured. Minutes before astronomers' instruments detected Supernova 1987A, a smattering of neutrinos given off by the dying star passed through neutrino detectors on Earth. Inset, above left: A computer shows which sensors detected the flash from a passing neutrino.

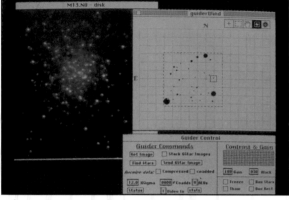

Top left: An astronomer of the 1920s photographs the Sun. Bottom left: A computer screen displays the view through a large telescope in a distant observatory. Future astronomers may not need to visit a telescope in order to view through it.

The People Who Keep Watch

Being an astronomer is fun, but it can be hard work. It may mean staying up all night to observe the skies and spending countless hours examining data for days, weeks, and even months on end.

Besides astronomers, there are others who keep watch on the skies. Technicians operate the scopes, handle the cameras, develop the films, analyze the light, and perform other tasks. What's more, in order to "see" above the thickest, dirtiest part of Earth's atmosphere, most large telescopes are on mountains. And because heating an observatory can make the air quiver and distort the image in the scope, workers often have to work in the cold night air.

If this sounds unpleasant, keep in mind that the excitement of making a new, important discovery makes all the hard work worthwhile.

Insets, opposite: far left: Opticians prepare to install the 40-inch (1-m) lens of the Yerkes Observatory in 1897. Left: Modern mirrors are larger, lighter, and easier to make than the Yerkes lens. Spinning furnaces can cast near-perfect mirrors.

Background, opposite: the mounting and dome of the Yerkes telescope.

Top: the 40-inch (1-m) refracting telescope at Yerkes Observatory in Wisconsin. It is now used for the careful measurement of star positions.

Bottom: the 136-inch (3.5-m) Apache Point Telescope. Astronomers can operate this telescope remotely by computer — without actually going to the observatory.

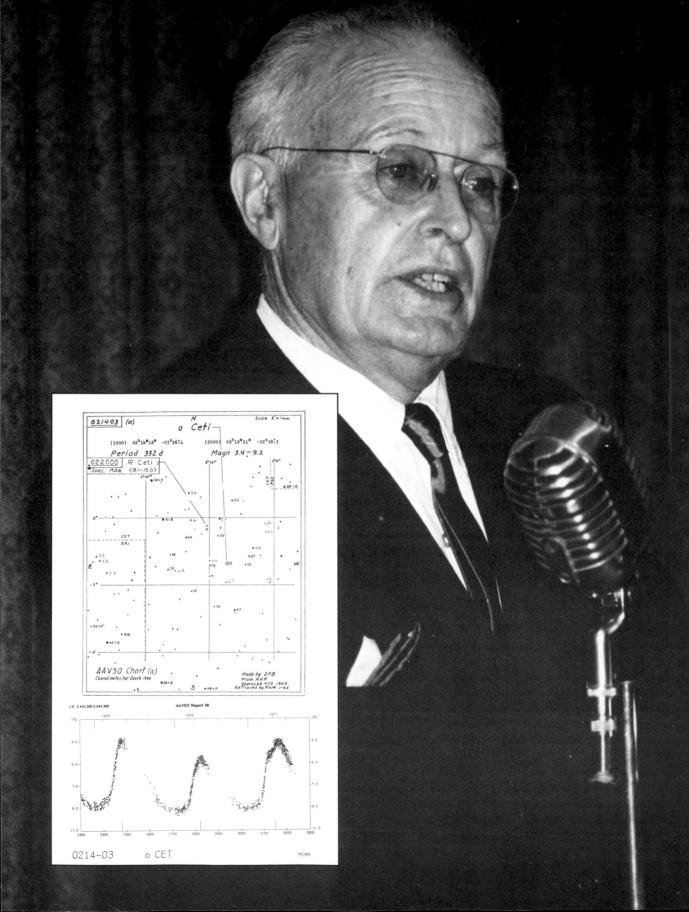

Back Yard Astronomers

Many professional astronomers with the latest instruments study distant galaxies and unusual objects in remote reaches of the cosmos. But what about our Sun, the Moon, the planets, and other objects closer to home?

There is no shortage of objects to observe in the sky, and many of those who look for these objects are amateurs. These people are not professionals, but they are fascinated by the sky. They keep looking at the sky night after night, recording their findings, taking photographs, and drawing sketches.

Amateur astronomers are often the ones who discover new comets, observe meteors, and keep track of stars that change in brightness. Sometimes they even spot a nova, a star that suddenly increases very much in brightness.

Opposite: Leslie Peltier, once called "the world's greatest nonprofessional astronomer." He discovered several comets and monitored stars that change brightness.

Inset, opposite: star chart (top) and plot of a star's changing brightness. Thousands of amateurs around the country contribute such observations of stellar behavior.

TWX 710 320 6842
ASTROGRAM CAM

BRADFIELD COMET BRADFIELD
19501 91224 79500 16190 13520
01059
20994 30769 BRADFIELD

This "astrogram" was sent to the Central Bureau for Astronomical Telegrams in 1950. It announces the discovery of a comet in 1949 by William Bradfield. Each word or cluster of numbers contains important data about the discovery, including the name of the discoverer, the object discovered, the name of the observer, the year of the announced location in the sky (1950), the date of the discovery (91224, for 1949, December 24), and other details of the observation.

**Astrograms —
spreading the cosmic news**

How does word get out when an astronomer spots a nova or discovers a new comet? Believe it or not, astronomers the world over send reports of every new astronomical discovery to telegram machines at the home of one person in Cambridge, Massachusetts. And from there, telegrams go _out_ to astronomers awaiting word of the latest discoveries. Even amateurs can send and receive "astrograms." Check page 30 of this book for more information.

Amateur Equipment

Amateurs don't have enormous telescopes or fancy equipment. But sometimes they make interesting observations with little more than a pair of high-quality binoculars.

Amateurs might also have telescopes that are small but of high quality, and sometimes they even make these telescopes themselves. Some amateurs have drives that make the telescope move in time with the way in which the sky turns.

Many amateurs have special cameras and computers. They have filters to be used in observing the Sun, and they often know exactly how to develop the photographs they take. Often, the best astronomical photographs — pictures of eclipses, for instance — are taken by amateurs.

Opposite, background and inset: amateur astronomer David Kriege at the eyepiece of the 25-inch (63.5-cm) telescope he constructed himself. At one time, a telescope of this size would have been available only to professional astronomers in an observatory.

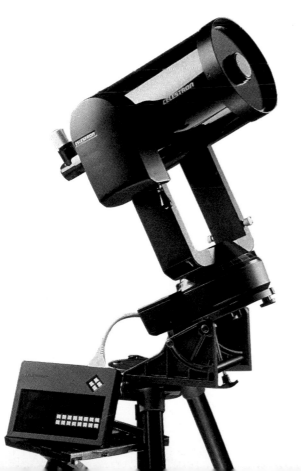

Lower left: a telescope that amateur astronomers can buy in a store. Its special features include a drive mechanism and a computer read-out.

Below: a photo of a total Solar eclipse taken by an amateur astronomer.

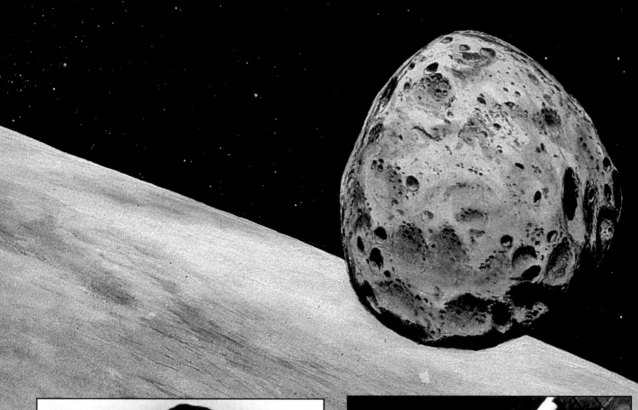

Amateur and Professional — The Fuzzy Line

Sometimes it's hard to tell the difference between an amateur astronomer and a professional astronomer.

One amateur, S. H. Schwabe, was a German pharmacist with a two-inch (five-cm) telescope. He liked to observe the Sun whenever he could, and he discovered the sunspot cycle in this way.

Asaph Hall was a carpenter who loved astronomy. He got a job at the Harvard Observatory as an assistant, and eventually he discovered the satellites of Mars.

Clyde Tombaugh was too poor to go to college, but he got a job as an assistant at Lowell Observatory, and eventually he discovered the planet Pluto!

Opposite: An artist imagines Phobos, one of the moons discovered by Asaph Hall, in orbit around Mars. Inset, far left: Asaph Hall, around 1870. Inset, left: the telescope Hall used to discover the Martian moons.

E. E. Barnard at Yerkes Observatory.

The most eagle-eyed astronomer of all?

It may have been US astronomer E. E. Barnard. In 1892, he discovered a small moon that was closer to Jupiter than any others known at the time. He could barely detect the satellite because it was so near Jupiter's bright light, but he saw it. Barnard also told a friend that he had seen a Moon-like crater on Mars. He thought he would be laughed at, so he didn't announce it. But in 1965, a probe took pictures of Mars, and there they were — craters.

Space Theory — Writing, Reading, Thinking

Astronomy takes equipment, patience, and luck. But it also takes a lot of thinking about science and mathematics.

Albert Einstein was not an astronomer, but he figured out an explanation of how gravity and other forces in the Universe might work. This explanation, called the general theory of relativity, has helped astronomers figure out what to look for in the cosmos. Einstein's theories have helped astronomers study unusual motions of planets. They have also helped astronomers look for strange things that happen to light, such as "gravitational lensing," which is the curving of light when it passes near a huge object like our Sun.

So far, everything astronomers have found has backed up Einstein's theories. Now there are theories about how the Universe came into existence, and astronomers must come up with observations that either back these theories or disprove them.

Opposite: a sculpture of Albert Einstein in Washington, DC. Einstein's studies helped explain the workings of gravity.

Below: an "Einstein ring," a cosmic mirage created when light from a distant galaxy bends as it passes by another galaxy.

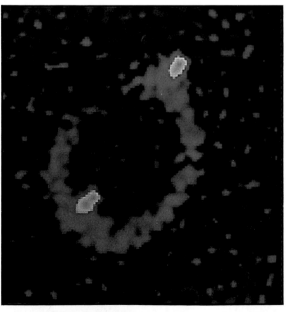

Gravitational lenses — throwing astronomers a curve

In 1936, Albert Einstein said that light from a distant star would curve around another star on its way toward us. We would thus see the distant star not as a <u>point</u> of light, but as a <u>ring</u> of light. This ring is called a "gravitational lens" or "Einstein ring." In 1988, half a century after Einstein had explained gravitational lensing, astronomers discovered that light from one quasar curves around a galaxy on its way to Earth and forms an Einstein ring.

We Don't Know It All!

Despite all the work with all the instruments, astronomers don't have all the answers. They don't know just how old the Universe is, or exactly how it came into existence, or just how it may have developed from a tiny object into the huge galaxy-filled Universe that now exists.

Most astronomers agree that the Universe is expanding, but they don't know if it will expand forever or start contracting again someday. There may be parts of the Universe we can't detect, but we don't know what these missing parts may be composed of.

Will we ever have all the answers? Probably not. For many people, not having all the answers seems itself to be a big problem. But then, problems make life more interesting, and they certainly make astronomy more exciting.

At dusk on a clear night, the dome of the McDonald Observatory's 107-inch (2.7-m) telescope opens to capture information streaming Earthward from the stars.

Fact File: The Spectrum and Modern Astronomy

We have all lived under the constant, reassuring glow of our Sun. Most of us know the Sun and such distant objects as the planets and stars as far-off sources of <u>visible, white</u> light. Most of us see their light with the naked eye; we also see it through optical telescopes.

But there's another form of visible light that we sometimes see — the spectrum. This is light refracted, or broken up, into the band of colors that together make up white light. We see the colors of the visible spectrum when sunlight is refracted as it passes through a glass prism, or through moisture in the air to produce a rainbow.

When white light is broken into its colors, it tells us more about a source of light than white light can by itself. For example, by examining the light of a distant galaxy with a special tool called a spectroscope, astronomers can figure out whether that galaxy is moving away from us or toward us — and how fast. Light waves of a body coming toward us are shorter, and move, or shift, toward the violet end of the spectrum. Light waves of a body moving away from us are longer, and shift toward the red end of the spectrum. So when Isaac Newton explained the visible spectrum — violet, blue, green, yellow, orange, and red — he opened the door to a whole new way of observing the Universe.

But there was more to come. Today, we know about other types of radiation, invisible to the human eye, that exist beyond the visible radiations, or colors, of the spectrum. For example, beyond the violet end of the spectrum lie ultraviolet radiation, x-rays, and gamma rays. And beyond the red end of the spectrum lie infrared radiation and radio waves.

All forms of radiation, including visible color, give off waves. These waves can be measured according to their different wavelengths. In astronomy, we detect these wavelengths with radio telescopes and other special instruments. By studying the information gathered by those instruments, we can learn about objects in deep space that we could never possibly visit, or even see, like black holes.

Today, we send rockets to collect information from other worlds. But the science of sky watching — astronomy — is still a visual science. This means it depends on gathering light from distant sources. Thanks to our detection of the visible and invisible spectrum, we know we can learn about the farthest reaches of the Universe without having to visit those places.

The Spectrum as a Tool of Modern Science — Names and Events

The Invisible Spectrum — Violet End

Explorer 42, launched from Kenya in 1970: discovered black holes in part because of their emissions of x-rays.

Cyril Hazard, Australian astronomer: in 1962 located a strong source of ultraviolet radiation with a huge red shift. This red shift indicated that the object — known as a quasar — was moving away from us at great speed and was therefore at a great distance from us. The nearest quasars are one billion light-years away!

Johann Wilhelm Ritter (1776-1810), German scientist: discovered ultraviolet radiation in tests performed on chemicals now used in making photographs.

The Visible Spectrum

Isaac Newton, English scientist (1642-1727): refracted white light through a prism into red, orange, yellow, green, blue, and violet — the spectrum. Was the first to explain light as a pattern of bright lines of different colors.

Joseph von Fraunhofer, German optician (1787-1826): developed a way of showing the spectrum more clearly, as a series of distinct vertical lines of color, as well as dark lines, called spectral lines. Combined the prism and the telescope into the spectroscope and used it to show that the spectral lines of the Moon and planets were the same as those of the Sun. This suggested, as we know today, that light from the Moon and planets is in fact reflected sunlight.

Robert Wilhelm Bunsen (1824-1899) and Gustav Robert Kirchoff (1824-1887), German scientists: used a burner developed by and named after Bunsen to determine that certain elements give off certain bright or dark lines. Therefore, light from a star can be analyzed to determine more than just brightness, position, and motion. Analysis can now determine chemical makeup as well.

Armand H. L. Fizeau (1819-1896), French scientist: in 1848 used a spectroscope to show whether an object was moving toward us (violet shift) or away from us (red shift) and how fast.

Annie Jump Cannon (1863-1941), US astronomer: used spectrographic methods to classify stars in orders of decreasing temperature.

Wilhelm Wien (1864-1928), German scientist: used the spectrum to measure stars' temperatures.

Vesto Melvin Slipher (1875-1969), US astronomer: discovered that most galaxies show a red shift, meaning that they are moving away from us. This discovery contributed toward the "Big Bang" theory of the birth of the Universe.

The Invisible Spectrum — Red End

William Herschel (1738-1822), German-born English astronomer: discovered infrared radiation by measuring heat beyond the red end of the spectrum and getting a <u>higher</u> temperature reading. This led to the conclusion that there must have been a line beyond red — infrared — that he couldn't see.

Heinrich Rudolph Hertz (1857-1894), German scientist: detected wavelengths much longer than infrared radiation — radio waves.

Karl Guthe Jansky (1905-1950), US radio engineer: detected a radio "hiss" that he discovered was coming from the center of our Galaxy. His discovery signaled the birth of radio astronomy.

Jocelyn Bell, British astronomer: in 1967 detected rapid pulses of radio waves from a star — the discovery of rapidly spinning, densely packed neutron stars, or pulsars.

More Books About Astronomy

Here are more books about astronomy. If you are interested in them, check your library or bookstore.

Ancient Astronomy. Asimov (Gareth Stevens)
Asimov on Astronomy. Asimov (Doubleday)
Astro-Dome Book: 3-D Map of the Night Sky. Hunig (Constellation)
Astronomy Basics. Litpak (Prentice-Hall)
Discovering the Stars. Santrey (Troll)
Eyes on the Universe: The History of the Telescope. Asimov (Houghton Mifflin)
Night Sky. Barrett (Franklin Watts)
The Space Spotter's Guide. Asimov (Gareth Stevens)

Places to Visit

You can explore the Universe without leaving Earth. Here are some museums, observatories, planetariums, and centers where you can stargaze and find many different kinds of space exhibits.

Hume Cronyn Observatory
University of Western Ontario
London, Ontario

Ronald E. McNair Space Theater
Russell Davis Planetarium
Jackson, Mississippi

Adler Planetarium
Chicago, Illinois

Dominion Astrophysical Observatory
Victoria, British Columbia

National Museum of Science
    and Technology
Ottawa, Ontario

Louisiana Arts and Science
    Center Planetarium
Baton Rouge, Louisiana

For More Information About Astronomy

Here are some people you can write to or call for more information about astronomy. Be sure to tell them exactly what you want to know about. And include your full name and address so they can write back to you.

For information about watching the skies:
Royal Astronomical Society of Canada
100 Queen's Park
Toronto, Ontario M5S 2C6, Canada

Royal Astronomical Society of Canada
1747 Summer Street
Halifax, Nova Scotia B3H 3A6, Canada

Astronomical "Hotline" for up-to-date descriptions of the sky:
Dial (416) 586-5751
The McLaughlin Planetarium
Toronto, Ontario

Canada-France-Hawaii Telescope
P. O. Box 1597
Kamuela, Hawaii 96743

**For information about sending an astronomical telegram
(see page 19 of this book):**
Central Bureau for Astronomical Telegrams
Smithsonian Astrophysical Observatory
60 Garden Street
Cambridge, Massachusetts 02138

Glossary

amateur: one who engages in an art, study, science, or sport for enjoyment rather than for money.

astronomy: the study of various bodies of the Universe.

atmosphere: the gases that surround a planet, star, or moon.

billion: in North America — and in this book — the number represented by 1 followed by nine zeroes — 1,000,000,000. In some places, such as the United Kingdom (Britain), this number is called "a thousand million." In these places, one billion would then be represented by 1 followed by 12 zeroes — 1,000,000,000,000: a million million, a number known as a trillion in North America.

black hole: an object in space caused by the explosion and collapse of a star. The object is so tightly packed that not even light can escape the force of its gravity.

calendar: a system for dividing time, most commonly into days, weeks, and months. Every calendar has a starting day and ending day for the year.

comet: an object made of ice, rock, and gas; has a vapor tail that may be seen when the comet's orbit brings it close to the Sun.

crater: a hole or pit on a planet or moon, created by volcanic explosions or the impact of meteorites.

galaxy: any of the many large groupings of stars, gas, and dust that exist in the Universe. Our galaxy is known as the Milky Way.

glacier: an enormous layer of ice formed from compacted snow, often itself carrying a layer of snow.

infrared radiation: "beneath the red" radiation. Infrared wavelengths are longer than red light wavelengths. Infrared is a form of invisible light, but you can feel infrared as heat.

nova: a star that suddenly increases greatly in brightness and returns to its original appearance in a few weeks, months, or years.

orbit: the path that one celestial object follows as it circles, or revolves, around another.

pharmacist: one who prepares and dispenses drugs.

probe: a craft that travels in space, photographing celestial bodies and even landing on some of them.

pulsar: a neutron star sending out rapid pulses of light or other radiation.

quasar: a "quasi-stellar," or "star-like," core of a galaxy that may have a large black hole at its center.

radio telescope: an instrument that uses a radio receiver and antenna both to see into space and to listen for messages from space.

radio waves: electromagnetic waves that can be detected by radio receiving equipment.

star cluster: a group of young, massive stars which will develop into isolated stars in only a few million years.

sunspot: a dark area on the Sun caused by gases that are cooler and shine less brightly than hot gases.

supernova: the result of a huge star exploding. When a supernova occurs, material from the star is spread through space.

telescope: an instrument usually made of lenses or mirrors to help us detect distant objects.

Universe: all existing things, including Earth and the Sun, Solar system, galaxies, and all that which is or may be beyond.

Index

The publishers wish to thank the following for permission to reproduce copyright and other material: front cover, pp. 8 (background), 10 (top inset), courtesy of Jet Propulsion Laboratory; p. 4 (large), © Greg Mort, 1984; p. 5 (bottom), courtesy of Wyoming Travel Commission; p. 5 (inset), from the collection of George G. Young; p. 6 (background), © Earl L. Kubis/ Tom Stack and Associates; p. 6 (insets), © California Association for Research in Astronomy; p. 7 (top), courtesy of Itek Optical Systems, in conjunction with the California Association for Research in Astronomy; p. 7 (bottom), © California Institute of Technology; p. 8 (insets), Space Telescope Science Institute; pp. 9 (top), 10 (center inset), Science Photo Libraries; p. 9 (bottom), © Fred Klein; p. 10 (background), © Mark Maxwell, 1988; pp. 10 (bottom inset), 15 (top), National Optical Astronomy Observatories; p. 11, © Royal Observatory, Edinburgh, 1986; pp. 12 (both), 13 (both), 25, © NRAO/AUI; p. 14 (background), photograph courtesy of Joe Stancampiano, Karl Luttrell, and the IMB Collaboration; p. 14 (top inset) courtesy of the IMB Collaboration; pp. 14-15 (bottom), © Rick Karpinski/DeWalt and Associates; pp. 16 (all), 17 (bottom), 23, Yerkes Observatory photographs; p. 17 (upper), © Leslie Bellavance, 1989; p. 18 (background), © Don Hurliss; p. 18 (inset), printed with special permission of Dr. Janet A. Mattei, Director of AAVSO; p. 20 (both), photographs by Matthew Groshek and Kate Kriege, © Gareth Stevens, Inc., 1989; p. 21 (left), courtesy of Celestron International; p. 21 (right), courtesy of NASA; p. 22 (background), © Joe Schabram, 1987; p. 22 (insets), official US Navy photographs; p. 24, courtesy of the National Academy of Sciences; p. 26, © The University of Texas McDonald Observatory; p. 29, photograph by Matthew Groshek, © Gareth Stevens, Inc., 1989.